BEARS

BEARS

LARGE AND NEEDY BEASTS
OF THE NORTH

AWESOME AT EVERYTHING

BY CHRISTA ROBERTS

CARTOON
NETWORK
B O O K S

AN IMPRINT OF PENGUIN RANDOM HOUSE

CARTOON NETWORK BOOKS
Penguin Young Readers Group
An Imprint of Penguin Random House LLC

Photo credits: cover: scenery (Purestock/Thinkstock), polar bear (michaklootwijk/iStock/Thinkstock), grizzly bear (seread/iStock/Thinkstock), panda (Jeannette Katzir/iStock/Thinkstock); back cover: polar bear (USO/iStock/Thinkstock), grizzly bear (OST/iStock/Thinkstock); panda (iStock/Thinkstock).

ISBN 9781101996157

10 9 8 7 6 5 4 3 2 1

Hey, what are you guys doing with my paper?

My name is Chloe Park. I'm a student at California University. People usually think I'm too young to be in college. It's true that I'm the youngest and smallest in my class (I skipped a couple of grades).

Ice Bear is setting the record straight.

Chloe, you're really, really, really smart.

For one of my classes, I did research on local bears. They're so interesting! I've learned a lot working on this assignment. Some of the stuff I learned was what I expected . . . but bears can surprise you!

That's right! We can. And we WILLLLLLLLLLLLLL!

Before I present my findings, let me back up and start from the very beginning. I knew I wanted to write about bears and went for a walk to see what I could find. It turned out to be my lucky day: I stumbled upon an actual bear cave!

Thankfully, I had my phone and a notebook with me.

3

Date: June 24

Time: Afternoon

Place: The bear's cave.

I peeked in the window and nobody was inside. There were bowls of porridge and melon rinds on the table, indicating that bears were close by. The cave was furnished with what looked like handmade furniture, and there was an open book on the table.

When we came home and found you, we were all really freaked out, you know?

I was filming the cave's interior when two bears opened the door. They startled me pretty badly! They were mad. And they weren't alone—another bear had been sleeping in the refrigerator the whole time. He came at me with an ax!

I shouted at the bears to stay back, but they tied me to a chair and dumped the contents of my backpack all over the floor. Typical bear stuff.

So not true. We were doing what any law-abiding bears would do when someone BREAKS INTO THEIR HOME.

Chloe called me "Surly." I don't know what that means. I'm going to pretend it means "Radical."

Ice Bear didn't want to call the police.

We weren't sure what was going on.

It turns out that the cave I found is the home of three bear brothers: Grizzly, Panda, and Ice Bear. I thought I was in serious danger at first, but once I started talking to them, they seemed to calm down.

Grizz started going through my backpack, tossing around my belongings, and eating my Honey Wasabi Gummies (note: write a case report on this later). Ice Bear tried to intimidate me by telling me he'd never seen a smaller human. (Hasn't he ever met a baby?) Then the bears started peppering me with questions.

Once the bears realized I wasn't there to hurt them, they let their guard down. And that's when I had my brilliant idea. I asked them if they'd mind if I hung around for a little bit to study their behavior.

 Whoa, hold up there a minute. TBH, we weren't so sure about this. No one had ever asked if they could study us before!

And then I made them an offer they couldn't refuse: I promised them as many gummies as they wanted.

HONEY WASABI GUMMIES: CATNIP FOR BEARS?

Believe it or not, Honey Wasabi Gummies are a highly desirable and addictive snack among bears. All three of my bear subjects could not resist this zingy treat.

In typical bear fashion, they first went through my belongings, foraging for food. When they found the gummies, Grizz started shoving entire pawfuls of them into his mouth.

I ordered him to spit them out immediately! I didn't want the bears to get sick. Honey Wasabi Gummies are pretty spicy. I can't eat more than one at a time. Grizz did not heed my warning, and the other two bears soon followed his lead. I don't think they are able to control themselves.

We worked so hard for those gummies. But now my tummy is hurting. Should have checked to see if they were safe to eat.

Oh my gosh, you guys! Those Honey Wasabi Gummies are SICK! I. Couldn't. Stop. Eating. Them. So good!!!! Yasssssss.

Ice Bear tried and failed to exhibit self-control.

After many days of careful observation, note taking, and documentation, I'm proud to present my findings in this report:

BEARS
Large and Needy Beasts of the North

A Case Study by Chloe Park

The topic of my report is . . . bears! In this carefully researched report, I located and studied three bear specimens of the Northern Californian region—Grizzly, Panda, and Polar Bear. I have compiled my facts about them to share with you in this book. First, let's get to know a little bit about each specimen.

Ice Bear has too many secrets.

Hey now. What did Chloe actually write about us? Let me see that. *Heh heh*, check out that cool photo. It's me. Got my swagger on . . .

Ugh—that's a horrible photo! This is super invasive! And "specimen" sounds so . . . scientific. We aren't specimens. We are BEARS.

At first it was pretty weird to have someone watching me eat and standing behind me while I brushed my teeth. But I got used to it. Before long I almost forgot Chloe was even there.

We read through Chloe's report. A lot of the stuff she had there just wasn't nice.

Ice Bear believed in Chloe.

It didn't represent us at all!

So, we're gonna correct any inaccuracies we find here. And add some things that

Everything in my report is true.

Chloe left out. This is our chance to show people who we really are. Chloe won't mind if we make a couple of adjustments.

We want to set the record straight . . . ON THE MOST IMPORTANT CREATURES EVER TO ROAM THE EARTH!!!!

BEARS

You thought you knew about bears . . . YOU DONT!!!!!!!!!!!!! Nothing can re-create the majesty of a bear overlooking his realm. More often than not, bears can be found saving the human race from themselves. Bears are also the cleanest of this planet's creatures; they bathe an astonishing three times a month. Bears have evolutionized to be masters of all combat.

> You can't put this in my report. It's made up.

Bears are the most incredible creatures

ever to walk the earth!

Go bears

Go bears

Go bears

Go bears

Bears are the champions of the world!

We are awesome . . . at everything!!!

Bears have more than eight abs, with
new abs being discovered every day!!!!!!!!!

Bears are buff.

BEARS
MAJESTIC
ACTION
HYGIENE
BRAZILIAN JIU-JITSU
FIRE
MAGIC
COMPETENT

Bears are more than just mascots.

Bears > Lions

Bears > Eagles

Bears > Panthers

Bears > Cougars

Bears > Tigers

Bears > Wildcats

Bears >>>>>>>>>>>>>>> EVERYBODY

IMPORTANT THINGS TO KNOW *about* GRIZZLY BEARS

I'm magnificent.

The term "grizzly" actually means "grayish," but people often associate it with the word "grisly," which means "inspiring horror or fear." And it's easy to understand why.

WHY? Why is it "easy"??????? That makes no sense. Bear discrimination at its finest. Wow. Been happening to us for years.

Grizzlies and mainland brown bears belong to the Ursidae family and are of the species *Ursus arctos* and subspecies *Ursus arctos horribilis.*

Ice Bear thinks that's a horrible name for bears.

Right? Why does it all have to be so complicated?

Because it's science.

Grizzlies eat plants and animals.

They avoid people.

They have a hard time climbing trees.

The force of their bite is super powerful.

Grizzly bears come in a lot of sizes and colors. They can be:

Brown (most common color)

Common = the BEST

Dark brown, sometimes with a silvery frosting on the back, i.e. "silvertip"

Black

Tan

Yellow

Off-white

Never seen an off-white Grizzly, but if Chloe says so, then . . .

My research says so.

A grizzly bear usually weighs between six hundred and eight hundred pounds. The bear that I observed never stopped eating, so I wouldn't be surprised if he weighed even more.

 Is she talking about me? So outrageous!

Oui. C'est tu.

IMPORTANT THINGS TO KNOW *about*
POLAR BEARS

They are carnivores.

They are normally found in cold areas such as the Arctic Circle.

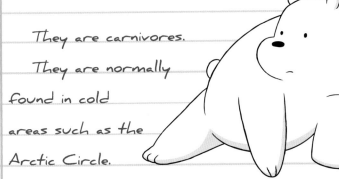

Polar bears are very large. They can be agile when stalking prey, such as seals. They are also good divers and swimmers. When a polar bear swims, you might only see his black nose and eyes.

Their favorite food? Seals.

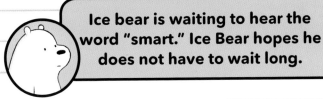

Ice bear is waiting to hear the word "smart." Ice Bear hopes he does not have to wait long.

Polar bears have something special—a white coat. This coat keeps them warm when they are out in snow and ice.

Male polar bears weigh 900–1,100 pounds, and female polar bears are about half of that.

I found out that Ice Bear is the baby brother of Grizzly and Panda. He's a bear of few words, but when he does speak, he usually says something that reflects his naturally good sense of humor and intelligence.

Ice Bear feels better now.

He's being modest. He's also an incredible chef and salsa dancer. He's also a martial arts artist. *Hiiiiiiii-yah!*

Ice Bear sleeps in the refrigerator. It keeps Ice Bear ice cool.

SHARK FANCY

Here is a special map I created to show native bear populations of the world.

 Uh, we cut out the map showing native bear populations because it was boring. We replaced it with this chill list.

Hey, I spent a lot of time making that map!

Get it? *Chill* list? HAHAHAHAHAHAHAHA!!!!! Bears are SO FUNNY!

HOW ICE BEAR CHILLS

In the fridge

At the ice rink

Thoughtfully and deliberately

In an ice bath

At the movie theater

With deep calming breaths

In his secret bathroom

IMPORTANT THINGS TO KNOW *about* PANDA BEARS

They are native to south central China. Panda bears belong to the Ursidae family, and are of the genus and species Ailuropoda melanoleuca.

Pandas are black and white. They have black fur on their ears, eye patches, muzzle, legs, and shoulders. The rest of the panda is white.

Black and white is so classic— my selfies are always cool!

Male pandas weigh about 250 pounds. Females weigh closer to 200.

Pandas eat a lot of bamboo (over 99% of their diet is bamboo!).

The PAN PAN

"MY SONG"
by Panda
Bamboo, you make me happy,
Bamboo, you make me smile,
Bamboo, you taste so tasty,
Bamboo, you've got
great style.

Don't be fooled by the panda bear's cuteness. A panda bear can be just as dangerous as any other bear.

What textbooks don't tell you is that Panda Bears have lots of feelings and that's a beautiful thing! We care deeply. Sometimes a bear needs to cry.

I DON'T WANT TO BE

PANDAFAN04329   7 Hours

770,783
PANDAFAN04329 Such a CUTIE-PATOOTIE! He's PURRRFECTLY delightful!

READ 928 COMMENTS

I LOVE YOU BEARY MUCH

THE CUTEST THING ON THE INTERNET!

Panda Bear is the second-oldest brother. Like most people I know, he spends a lot of time on his phone. As in, it never leaves his side. He is constantly taking selfies and using social media apps.

ABOUT

☺ MALE

🏠 FOREST

💍 SINGLE

👤 224

(I don't think he likes to admit it, but it's obvious that he wants a girlfriend very badly. I discovered that Panda has joined a number of dating sites. I can tell he has a good heart, but he seems to get embarrassed easily. I don't think he has as much confidence as his brothers.)

I admit it. I do want a girlfriend. And my confidence isn't the greatest. That's why I repeat this three times every morning and every night:

Panda is smart.

Panda is worthy.

Panda is the greatest at everything.

Panda is the Man.

A DAY IN THE LIFE OF A BEAR

After observing the bears for many days, it became clear that bears spend most of their time sleeping and eating. When they aren't sleeping or eating, they are often resting or looking for food.

 We like to have fun, too! We play games and watch TV and listen to music.

 Ice Bear masters new recipes.

I take drawing lessons twice a week!

Eating and sleeping is only a small part of what we do. My life is FULL.

Bears are entrepreneurial. We run small businesses!

#bears #foodtrucks #thecalzonelife

 I don't think this applies to all bears.

PANDA

Chloe had a really boring page here about Mammals of the Nearctic Realm. Hit Delete! This is much more useful:

Hey, I spent a lot of time researching that.

Panda's Tips for Meeting Quality Partners Online

No one knows better than me that it can be hard to meet quality people. I'm a busy guy, so when I use social media, I want results. Online dating can be great, but you have to know what you're doing or

you can get in hot water—or just waste a lot of time.
Here are my top tips for social romancing success.

1. Show them your good side! Make sure your
profile picture looks attractive, confident, and cool.
Lighting, pose, expression—it all matters. If a girl
can't see what you really look like, she's not going to
want to meet you. And if you look
like a weirdo in your picture,
she *really* won't want to
meet you. Don't use a
super-old photo of
yourself, or an artsy,
blurry photo where it's
hard to tell what you really
look like. And remember to
smile! I went through 748
selfies before I found the

right one. Don't be afraid to ask your friends for their opinions. My two bros helped a lot. They tried to pretend like they weren't interested, but I could tell they cared.

2. Check out your potential match's profile. Do you think the two of you would get along? I mean, obviously you're great (LOLZ), but you need to be the kind of bear that she's looking to meet. Romancing is a two-way street. If the person you like doesn't like you back, MOVE ON, BRO.

3. Ask good questions, like these:

• What do you do for fun?

• Do people think you are fun?

• Are you funny?

• How many times a day do you eat?

• What is your favorite food?

• Are you a good cook?

• Which do you like better: veggie pizza or cheesy enchiladas? Why?

• What is your favorite anime series?

4. Don't be a stalker. As a wise bear once said: "A watched pot never boils." It's true. If you sit and wait for a reply, it will take FOREVER. Quit hitting the refresh button and get on with your life, bro. Then, when she replies to your message, it will be a happy surprise.

LIVING ENVIRONMENT

As you might imagine, bears are not the neatest creatures. I had the chance to observe them in their natural habitat. Frankly, it was a pigsty. Or maybe I should call it a "bearsty." There were clothes and socks strewn all over the floor, empty food wrappers and takeout containers on the table, and mounds of crusted-over pots and pans. There was also a really bad smell that an entire can of Powder Flower Room Freshener couldn't disguise.

If Chloe is so smart, she should know that creative souls sometimes might be a little messy. So we left our plates on the table. So what? We have more important things to worry about. Like LOVE.

Ice Bear stands behind his position on cleanliness.

Ice Bear believes in the KonMari method of decluttering.

Hey, wait up, here. We are very good at being neat. We just don't always want to be neat.

"An Ode to Awesomeness"
by Grizz

Everyone is awesome. Especially Bears.

We have fur.

We have fun.

We have friends.

Life wouldn't be the same without bears.

I wouldn't be the same if I wasn't a bear.

If anyone tells me I am not awesome, I tell them:

Dude! I'm a bear!

BRO CHORES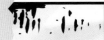

GRIZZ

Monday: Rest

Tuesday: Yard work

Wednesday: Rest

Thursday: Rest

Friday: Plan awesome weekend fun

Saturday: Host party

Sunday: Rest

Pruning the bushes really takes it out of you! That's why I need so much rest.

PANDA

Monday: Make grocery wish list

Tuesday: Rest

Wednesday: Fold laundry

Thursday: Rest

Friday: Do internet surveys for money

Saturday: Attend party

Sunday: Rest

Friday is Ice Bear's favorite day of the week.

ICE BEAR

Monday: Grocery shopping, cook dinner

Tuesday: Clean bathroom, cook dinner

Wednesday: Do laundry, cook dinner

Thursday: Vacuum living room, cook dinner

Friday: Rest

Saturday: Run errands, cook dinner

Sunday: Clean up party, cook dinner

HYGIENE

The bear's powerful stench can alert passersby to its presence, particularly if one is upwind.

Powerful stench?! It's an alluring musk!

Ice Bear smells like clean babies.

Biggest offenders:

Breath

Fur

Armpits

Butt

45

BEAR STACK!

Are you familiar with a bear stack? I wasn't either. It's when the bears stand—or "stack"— on top of one another. Ice Bear goes on the bottom, then Panda, with Grizz on top. It's their own unique way of getting around! (It's also so cute! Brotherly bear bonding!)

In our bear stack:

1. We can reach the cereal boxes on the top shelf at the grocery store.

2. We can wash windows.

3. We can rescue kittens stuck in trees.

4. We can wave to people on the top level of a double-decker bus.

5. We can make birds feel less lonely.

6. We can scare away an entire pack of wolves.

SOCIAL IGNORANCE

Bears are very smart. They teach each other things, such as how to get food, how to get along with others, or where a good place to take a nap might be. However, bears have difficulty adjusting to social situations and tend to make those around them uncomfortable.

We don't make people uncomfortable!

Case study #1: I accompanied the bears to one of their favorite restaurants in Chinatown. Instead of waiting for menus, the bears climbed over the food cart and began grabbing at the containers of rice and dumplings. People around us looked alarmed and annoyed. It was a little embarrassing.

Embarrassing??? We can't help it—we love that place!

Case study #2: Panda uses cutlery to scratch his back. Who does that? And no surprise, this social faux pas gets him a lot of weird looks.

What can I say? I'm itchy.

Case study #3: Ice Bear growls at kids if they don't move out of his way. I don't think he would really hurt anybody, but the kids don't know that! They usually run away.

A mirror has been held up to Ice Bear's poor behavior. Ice Bear will do better.

Chronic halitosis

Poor teeth can worsen
a cranky disposition

One-track mind

Frequently flails
arms around

Fur usually
unwashed

Insatiable black
hole—never
stops eating

Large
hindquarters

Feet small in proportion; trips often

51

ICE BEAR

A Wellness Routine
by Ice Bear

10 minutes of deep breathing

45 minutes of yoga sequences

15 minute herbal tea break

30 minutes of karate practice

20 minutes of meditation

Did you know that BEARS are athletes?
Well, we ARE. And there's a reason for our
bear stack. Here are some of the athletic
things we bears can do.

We triple spike the volleyball.
We climb the rock wall super fast.
We Hula-Hoop three hoops at once.
We catch the ball with three sets of paws.
We score the winning basket EVERY time.

THE BEARS' TV HABITS

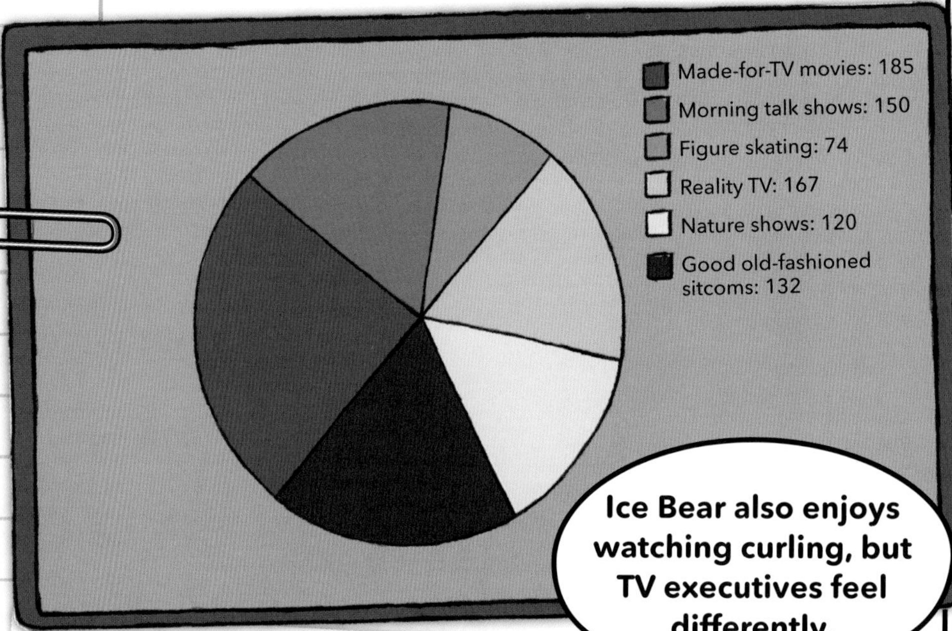

- ■ Made-for-TV movies: 185
- ■ Morning talk shows: 150
- ■ Figure skating: 74
- ■ Reality TV: 167
- □ Nature shows: 120
- ■ Good old-fashioned sitcoms: 132

Ice Bear also enjoys watching curling, but TV executives feel differently.

PANDA

LOG DROP LODGE

Shout-out for our brother, Pan-Pan! Keeping it black and white for more than ten years!

Great Things That Are Black and White by Panda

- Black-and-white cookies
- Chessboards
- Newspapers
- Penguins

- Pianos
- Dice
- Pandas
- Tuxedos

ICE BEAR'S PROPERTY DAMAGE OVER TIME

DAMAGE

Ice Bear
Wakes Up

Ice Bear settled that out of court.

12AM 1 2 3 4 5 6 7 8 9 10 11 12PM 1 2 3

ICE BEAR

"A Haiku"
by Ice Bear

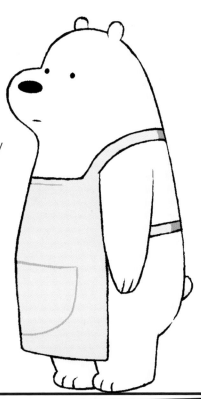

Drum beat in kitchen

My knife is sharp and ready

I cut the sushi

WHAT MOTIVATES A BEAR?

Bears will do most anything for food—it's their main motivation.

> **Let me repeat that. "Bears will do most anything for food—it's their main motivation."** *Anything for food??????* **That's just not true. I don't understand. This is just a misrepresentation.**

Most bears stay inside their dens for the winter. Because their access to food depends on the seasons, bears have ravenous appetites. They eat practically nonstop.

Firsthand examples:

Grizz will lie around and eat ALL DAY LONG if given the opportunity

To be fair, I only do that on Sunday, Monday, Wednesday, Thursday, and Friday. *HA!!*

Panda gets so hungry he needs all four burners on the stove to keep up with his appetite.

I mean, geez! What can I say? I'm a growing bear!

Unfortunately, Ice Bear has resorted to criminal activity to keep up with his appetite. I witnessed him smashing the window of a seafood shop with his ax in order to grab some halibut.

Ice Bear feels shame.

HIERARCHY

Hierarchy is a ranking of authority. It's important to understand that bears live in a dominance hierarchy. This is determined by several factors, including a bear's size, age, and personality.

Grizz is a grizzly bear. He's the clear leader of the bear brothers. He is also the oldest. From my time spent observing him, I can tell that he likes to have fun. He's got a great sense of style—he wears rad sunglasses! He likes to meet new people and is pretty friendly with everyone he meets. His social awareness is a little lacking, though, and his enthusiasm for life sometimes gets him into trouble. One thing that surprised me was that he raps!

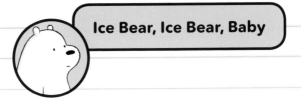

Ice Bear, Ice Bear, Baby

GRIZZ

"A Rap" by Grizz

My name is Grizz.

My soda's gotta fizz.

When I go out,

the deets are my bizz.

My brothers are my boyz.

They always got my back,

If you see us,

Come and join the bear stack.

Yeah. [Drop mic.]

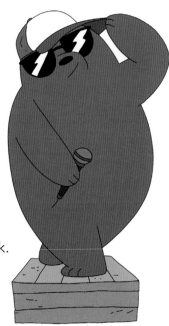

Grizz has always been our leader. Even when we were little, he always knew exactly what to do. We'd still be in a cardboard box on the side of the road if it weren't for him. I love you, Grizz!

Ice Bear knows his strengths. Where he has weakness, he looks to his brother, Grizz.

It's my job to keep this family in tip-top shape. I take my duties as the older brother very seriously. I'm older. Stronger. More experienced. I am . . . the leader of the pack.

EXPRESSIONS

 Bears can be very expressive. We show our emotion in different ways.

Here is an example of being sad:

Here is an example of being mad:

Here is an example of being uncomfortable:

Here is an example of being hungry:

Here is an example of being happy:

If you accidentally stumble upon a bear, try to make yourself look as big as possible. That's because—

Oh my gosh, this is just more lies! So inaccurate! Bears are the ones who have to make themselves look larger and more intimidating. This one time wolves tried to attack me and I lifted my backpack over my head and scared them away. I saved the day!

Ice Bear wishes he knew how to do that. He has tried. And failed.

Things you can stand on in the woods to make yourself look bigger and scarier:

- tree stump
- chair
- picnic table
- cooler
- rock
- your bros

PANDA

Bonjour!

If there's one place I've always wanted to visit, it would be the City of Lights . . . Paris!

There is so much there to see and do . . . and eat! *Ooh la la,* a trip to Paris is on my bucket list, and when I go there, here is what I will do:

- Cruise down the Seine on one of the *Bateaux-Mouches.* At night. With a pretty French lady. Sigh.

- Eat a pastry from every bakery in Paris. It might take a while, but it can be done!

- Get a selfie with the *Mona Lisa* at the Louvre.

- Take a food tour with my brothers.

- Enjoy the view from the top of the Eiffel Tower.

  I'm a little nervous about being up that high, but you only live once!

- Speak French all the time. *Oui! Non! Pamplemousse!*

- Check out the gargoyles at Notre-Dame Cathedral.

- Check out the French electronica scene.

- Take a nap in the Luxembourg Gardens.

- Fall in love and get a girlfriend. A bear can dream . . .

Online Dating Sites
to Check Out
by Panda

eBear.com

Plenty of Bears

HoneyBear.com

Not Your Basic Bear

Share & Care

Forest Friends

Walk in the Woods

Let Your Claws Down

Sugarbear.com

Hibernating Honeys

BDate

Forest Fire

PHYSICAL ACTIVITY

Some days, the bears were really active. They'd take a walk, play a game of pick-up basketball, or practice martial arts in the park. On other days, though, all they did was lie around their bear cave and eat. On a scale of 1–5 with 5 being the most amount of activity possible, I'd say they average a 2.5. I'm going to see what I can do to encourage them to stay fit.

Ice Bear is committed to staying strong in mind and body.

HIBERNATION

Bears adapt to the winter season's shortage of food by hibernating. Not all kinds of bears hibernate, but black bears, brown bears, and grizzly bears do. If you saw a bear in hibernation, you might think it was just asleep. A bear's heart rate slows down so much that it doesn't burn energy nearly as fast as it does while it's awake.

Okay, Chloe is right about this. Believe it or not, I hadn't even heard of hibernation until recently. But now that I have, I think it's a great idea. I mean, you get to eat a ton of food and sleep all you want. What could be better?

Hibernation List:

Food   Pillows   Mattresses

Ambient music   Blankets   Towels

ORAL HYGIENE

It's no surprise that bears have really bad breath. They eat everything! Berries. Tree roots. Fish. Bamboo. Bark. BUGS. It's kind of disgusting when you think about it.

Ice Bear suggests you don't think about it.

Observations:

• Food all over bear cave, wrappers on the floor, empty cans on the table, crumbs everywhere

• Dental floss on bathroom sink looked unused

• Toothbrushes

• No mouthwash

*Note: when I first met Grizz, I got the chance to look inside his mouth. His teeth looked yellowed and sharp, and there was a lot of slobber. His breath was awful. Still, it was fascinating.

Based on what I observed, it's true what the scientists say about bears' oral hygiene. The number of Grizz's cavities was downright atrocious.

Ah, here we go again. That is SO NOT TRUE! I mean, yes, we eat some weird things but I always brush my teeth before I go to bed. I use a special toothpaste that's guaranteed to give me fresh breath AND a healthier smile.

Ice Bear needs to floss more.

I make sure to use mouthwash every day. You never know who you might want to talk to!

ASIAN FOOD

One thing that might surprise you is that bears really, really like Asian food. Especially dim sum.

Okay, Chloe *finally* got a detail right. Seriously? I love vegetable dumplings. Finely shredded carrot, chopped shiitake mushrooms, and some sweet cabbage . . . a dumpling is a little pillow of loveliness on my tongue. Let's order out, guys!

Yeah, let's do it! We can get that spicy garlic sauce we got last time. Oh, man, I've been dreaming about that for days.

Ice Bear will hang up his apron tonight.

TAKEOUT RECEIPT FROM DIM SUM GARDEN

Steamed Vegetable Dumplings
—10 orders

Sautéed Vegetable Delight
—4 orders

Kung Pao Bean Curd
—2 orders

Snow Peas with Water Chestnuts
—2 orders

Chinese Baby Eggplant in Garlic Sauce
—5 orders

Vegetable Moo Shu
—9 orders

Extra Garlic Sauce

Extra Soy Sauce

Extra Fortune Cookies
(50)

Now then. Anybody up for ordering a pepperoni pizza?

Sorry if we got a little sauce on this page. We didn't have enough napkins.

Who needs a stupid section on reference material? This is what's important. This is what's REAL.

Did you know that all these things were invented by BEARS?

Airplanes	Computers
Cars	Penicillin
Submarines	Personal computers
Televisions	Happiness
Bear emoji	Summertime
Printing press	Cannoli

MY FAME SHALL LIVE ON!

This is what Chloe should have written in the first place.

Bears are law-abiding citizens. There is no reason to be afraid of bears. There are so many ways that bears contribute goodness to the world we can't even count them. We tried to count them anyway, because we don't give up. Why? Because WE ARE BEARS.

1. We are spiritual.
2. We are magical.
3. We are competent.
4. We like campfires.
5. People like to take photos of us.
6. We're fun.
7. We have a constellation named after us which means WE ARE STARS.
8. We are every kid's favorite stuffed animal.
9. We are majestic.
10. We are bears.

I'm going to get an "F" on this paper.

As I worked on this presentation, I realized that people don't know as much about bears as they think they do. People constantly asked me questions about my findings, and I was surprised at how many misconceptions there are about bears. I decided to let the bears address these fallacies themselves.

Q. Are bears dogs?

We are not dogs. I'm honestly embarrassed for you that you had to ask.

If you want Ice Bear to share his secrets, please do not call him a dog.

Q. Is there an evolutionary benefit for bears to have such big behinds?

Our butts look awesome!

I posted a great selfie the other day with my butt in it. It got three hundred likes! That seems like a pretty good benefit to me.

Ice Bear doesn't feel uncomfortable being subjected to the human gaze.

Q. Bears are so hefty. They often move really slowly, right?

Hey, that's not nice! How'd you like to be called hefty?

We can run as fast as a horse. That means we can outrun you!

GRIZZ

Working Out with the Grizz

Some people (*ahem*, Chloe) think that bears

lounge around all day. THIS IS TOTALLY WRONG

AND A BIG LIE. Okay, sure, we might do that every

now and then, but we spend a lot of time exercising.
We jog through the woods. We climb trees. We play
lots of basketball. We do all sorts of stuff. I make

sure to give lots of encouragement to my bros. I say
things like *whoo! oh, yeah! nice job, bros!* and *tally-
ho!* It really helps. Most of all, I make sure everyone
drinks plenty of water. A hydrated bear is a happy
bear!

A WORD OF CAUTION

Remember, bears are wild animals. They can be dangerous and unpredictable. Bears have been known to hurt and even kill people. It's best to avoid them if at all possible.

Bears are so not dangerous. That is just a myth! We want to be friends with everybody and live together in peace. Don't try to surprise or threaten us and we'll all get along. Nobody likes that.

Keep your distance from bears.

If a bear approaches you, do not run. Instead, try to make yourself look as big as possible.

Ice Bear thinks it's strange when people wave their arms and talk loudly to bears. You will never be as tall as a bear, so don't even try.

I don't like it when people back away slowly from me. It hurts my feelings. Bears think deeply about things.

If you are attacked by a bear, it means the bear sees you as prey. You will have to fight back as hard as you can. Use any object you can find to help you fight—branches, backpacks, walking sticks.

Branches? Sticks? Who do you think we are? Why you gotta be so mean?

FOODS BEARS REALLY LIKE

Gummies

Soup

Cheese puffs

Sushi

Fish

Kale

Scrambled eggs

Spicy stuff

Donuts

Peanut butter and jelly sandwiches

Spaghetti and meatballs

Cheesecake

Danish

Tacos

Basically everything

IF YOU ARE CAMPING, KEEP THESE RULES IN MIND:

Never leave your food unattended. When you have finished eating, all of your trash should be placed in bear-proof dumpsters. Any food that is left over should be placed back in a container and stored inside your vehicle. Don't leave the windows open!

Bear-proof dumpsters. So insulting.

Don't throw food or trash into a campfire. And never feed a bear. That is a big mistake.

Anybody got anything spicy for me?

A little note about "bear coolers" from your friends, AKA, the people who know about stuff like this . . . THE BEARS.

A MEMO TO PEOPLE EVERYWHERE, ESPECIALLY PEOPLE WHO GO CAMPING.

There is no bear-resistant cooler. It is a mythical product that cooler companies want you to believe exists so you will buy more coolers. It's the same thing with squirrel-proof bird feeders. Have you seen a squirrel? Those guys are sneaky.

Bears are very intelligent! We can absolutely figure out how to pick cooler locks. Don't think that we can't.

Ice Bear knows this is truth.

Without BEARS there would be a lot of great stuff missing from the world.

There would be no BEAR conditioning.
There would be no BEAR packages.
There would be no BEAR salons
There would be no street BEARS.

The world would be a really lonely and boring place without bears there to make it awesome.

BEAR APPEARANCE

Bears have very small ears and eyes in relation to their gigantic heads. Don't be deceived, though—their eyesight is as good as a human's, and they have excellent night vision. Bears spend a lot of time stopping to sniff the air because their sense of smell is so strong that they can smell food miles away.

 Now that's more like it! Bears are the best.

Bears have very, very large butts. They have five digits on each foot. When they walk, they place their entire foot on the ground. They have strong claws.

 That sounds . . . cool?

GRIZZ

Baby Bears

Bears have excellent memories. We remember EVERYTHING. When we were baby bears, we really wanted somebody to adopt us. We lived at

a pet shop and tried to look as cute as possible so somebody would take us home. We even made a commercial, but it just didn't happen.

Pan-Pan was so sad. He didn't want to leave the pet shop and go into the harsh, outside world. I told him to focus on the Vision Wall—all the wonderful things out there waiting for us. The Vision Wall inspired us to dream big and work to make our dreams come true.

The owner of the pet shop eventually put us into a cardboard box and threw us in the trash. Like garbage! That made us sad, but it didn't stop us. We dusted ourselves off and started walking down the street.

But guess what? A lot of people saw the commercial, and they wanted to adopt us!

They gave us new names. I was Spike. My li'l bro was now Fabio. And Panda was Mr. Sprinkles.

Being adopted wasn't what I thought it would be. Sure, it was great getting pizza. And my new owner was nice. But I missed my bros too much. I couldn't stand it. I ran back to the pet shop and, thankfully, was able to reunite with my brothers.

My family.

FAMOUS BEARS OF THE WORLD

Prince Beary

Beary Styles

Maria von Bear

Bear Jordan

Beary Seinfeld

Beary Potter

Beary Bonds

Bearlie Chaplin

IN CONCLUSION

After careful research and observation, I learned a lot about bears. But in the end, maybe the most important thing that happened was that I got three new friends.

Grizz, Ice Bear, Panda . . . you guys are awesome at everything. I love you.

 Finally. Words we can all agree on. GO BEARS!